I DON'T CARE!

LEARNING ABOUT BAD HABITS

Katherine Eason

FOX EYE
PUBLISHING

Jack had some **BAD HABITS**.
He **BIT HIS FINGERNAILS**
and **PICKED AT HIS SCABS**.
Sometimes, he **PICKED HIS NOSE**.

Jack **DIDN'T CARE** about his bad habits. He didn't think that they mattered.

On the school bus, Jack sat next to his friend. Jack had a scab on his knee.

The scab felt itchy and sore. Jack **PICKED HIS SCAB**. That made it bleed. It was a **BAD HABIT**.

At school, Nurse Nula put a plaster on Jack's knee.

Next, Jack **PICKED HIS NOSE**. Then, his nose bled. It was a **BAD HABIT**. Miss Book took Jack to the nurse's office.

Nurse Nula said that picking your nose can cause a **NOSEBLEED**.

At home, Jack told Dad what had happened at school. Dad told Jack that keeping his hands busy would help him to **STOP** his **BAD HABITS**. He gave Jack a fidget bracelet.

Dad asked Jack if he thought it was important to stop his bad habits. Jack thought about his bleeding knee. He thought about how his fingers had hurt. He thought about his nosebleed. Perhaps stopping **BAD HABITS** mattered after all.

The next day, Jack wore the fidget bracelet. He didn't pick his scabs or bite his fingernails. He didn't pick his nose, too.

Jack drew a picture for Nurse Nula. She smiled. Jack had learnt to **CONTROL** his **BAD HABITS**, and it **FELT GOOD!**

Words and Behaviour

Jack had bad habits in this story and that caused a lot of problems.

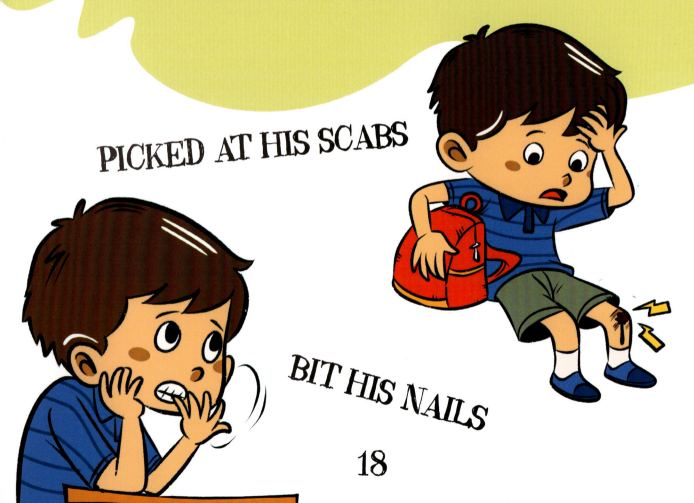

PICKED AT HIS SCABS

BIT HIS NAILS

There are a lot of words to do with bad habits in this book. Can you remember all of them?

PICKED HIS NOSE

Let's talk about feelings and manners

This series helps children to understand difficult emotions and behaviours and how to manage them. The characters in the series have been created to show emotions and behaviours that are often seen in young children, and which can be difficult to manage.

I Don't Care!

The story in this book examines the reasons for controlling bad habits. It looks at why stopping bad habits is important and how stopping bad habits stops people from harming themselves.

How to use this book

You can read this book with one child or a group of children. The book can be used to begin a discussion around complex behaviour such as having bad habits.

The book is also a reading aid, with enlarged and repeated words to help children to develop their reading skills.

How to read the story

Before beginning the story, ensure that the children you are reading to are relaxed and focused.

Take time to look at the enlarged words and the illustrations, and discuss what this book might be about before reading the story.

New words can be tricky for young children to approach. Sounding them out first, slowly and repeatedly, can help children to learn the words and become familiar with them.

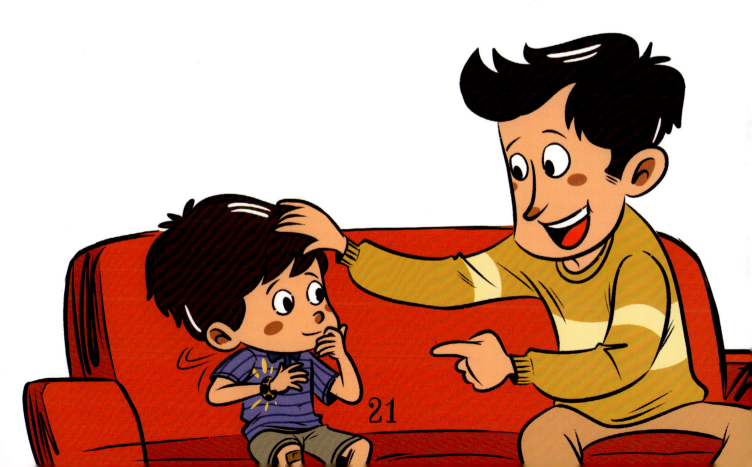

How to discuss the story

When you have finished reading the story, use these questions and discussion points to examine the theme of the story with children and explore the emotions and behaviour within it:
- What do you think the story was about?
- Have you been in a situation in which you had bad habits? What was that situation?
- Do you think bad habits don't matter? Why?
- Do you think controlling bad habits is important? Why?
- What could go wrong if you do not control bad habits?

Titles in the series

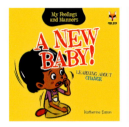  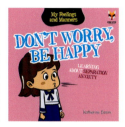 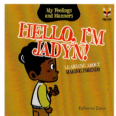 
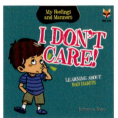  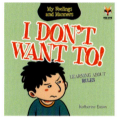 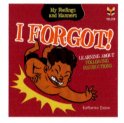 
   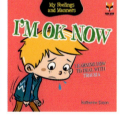 
   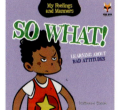 

First published in 2023 by Fox Eye Publishing
Unit 31, Vulcan House Business Centre,
Vulcan Road, Leicester, LE5 3EF
www.foxeyepublishing.com

Copyright © 2023 Fox Eye Publishing
All rights reserved. No portion of this book may be reproduced in any form without permission from the publisher, except as permitted by U.K. copyright law.

Author: Katherine Eason
Art director: Paul Phillips
Cover designer: Emma Bailey
Editor: Jenny Rush

All illustrations by Novel

ISBN 978-1-80445-174-8

Printed in China